QUOTIVATE:

Words to Create Your Positive Life

Cys Bronner

To request permissions, contact the publisher at:
Cys.Bronner@ActionSteps4Success.com

Paperback ISBN: 9798598514467

Credits:
Joshua Rittenhouse (Editor)
Cys Bronner (Book Cover & Author)

Published by:
ActionSteps4Success, LLC
9903 Santa Monica Blvd, 812
Beverly Hills, CA 90212
ActionSteps4Success.com

Disclaimer: This publication is meant as a source of
valuable information for the reader, however it is not
meant as a substitute for direct expert assistance. If such
level of assistance is required, the services of a competent
professional should be sought. The information in this
book was correct at the time of publication, but the
Author does not assume any liability for loss or damage
caused by errors or omissions.

*To my parents, Stanley and Regina Bronner;
whose "Bronnerisms" filled my world with
positive words, actions and encouragement.*

Table of Contents

Quotational!

"People who make no mistakes lack boldness and the spirit of adventure. They are the brakes on the wheels of progress."
— *Dale E. Turner*

"Many an exhausted high achiever has reached a lofty goal only to discover that it was a false peak, that the true summit loomed much higher. Others have reached the highest heights only to find them barren and empty and then realized the only way down was...down. Yet many a modest achiever has trekked through a lifetime of rocky trails and boggy swamps to realize, after all, what a glorious and rewarding trip it has been."
— *Dr. Ivan Misner*

"Parkinson's Law: Expenses always rise to meet income. This is why most people retire poor. To become wealthy, you must spend less than you earn, and save the balance."
— *Brian Tracy*

"listening tip: Be present and fully engaged — don't multitask."
— *Mike Robbins*

"Ability is of little account, without opportun-ity."
— *Lucille Ball*

"Take one full day off every week. During this day, absolutely refuse to read, clear correspondence, catch up on things from the office, or do anything else that taxes your brain."
— *Brian Tracy*

"Don't judge each day by the harvest you reap, but by the seeds you plant."
— *Robert Louis Stevenson*

"Impossible is a word to be found only in the dictionary of fools."
— *Unknown*

"If you're going through hell, keep going."
— *Sir Winston Churchill*

Your Morning Quota

"Good morning. Life is like a mirror: it will smile at you if you smile at it"

"Every morning has a new beginning, a new blessing, a new hope. It's a perfect day because it's God's gift. Have a blessed, hopeful day to begin with."

"Today will be a good day, so wake up and smile."

"Set a goal that makes you want to jump out of bed in the morning."

"I opened two gifts this morning. They were my eyes."

"Life without a purpose is a languid, drifting thing; every day we ought to review our purpose, saying to ourselves, this day let me make a sound beginning."
  – *Thomas Kempis*

"Good morning is not just a word. It's an action and a belief to live the entire day well. Morning is the time when you set the toe for the rest of the day. Set it right. Have a nice day."

"Something special awaits you each day. All you need is to recognize it and make the most of it. Have a positive attitude throughout the day and then that today is going to be the best day in your life. Good morning."

"Although time seems to fly, it never travels faster than one day at a time. Each day is a new opportunity to live your life to the fullest. In each waking day, you will find scores of blessing and opportunities for positive change. Do not let your today be stolen by the unchangeable past or the indefinite future! Today is a new day! Good morning."

— *Steve Maraboli*

"Life laughs at you when you are unhappy. Life smiles at you when you make others happy."

— *Charlie Chaplin*

"It doesn't matter what day of the week it is. As long as we are together, it will always be a beautiful day."

"The world is beautiful outside when there is stability inside."

"Your journey will be much lighter and easier if you don't carry your past with you."

"When you arise in the morning, think of what a precious privilege it is to be alive, to breathe, to think, to enjoy, to love."

— *Marcus Aurelius*

"Waking up this morning, I smile. 24 brand new hours are before me. I vow to live each fully in each moment."

— *Thich Nhat Hanh*

"Morning is an important time of day because how you spend your morning can often tell you what kind of day you are going to have."
 -- *Lemony Snicket*

"Prayer is the key of the morning and the bolt of the evening."
 -- *Mahatma Gandhi*

"Not only the day but all things have their morning."
 -- *French Proverb*

"An early-morning walk is a blessing for a whole day"
 -- *Henry David Thoreau*

"Life is too short, she panicked, I want more. He nodded slowly, Wake up earlier."
 -- *Dr. SunWolf*

"You cry and scream and you stomp your feet and you shout. You say: "You know what" I'm giving up, I don't care!" And then you go to bed and you wake up and it's a brand new day. And you pick yourself up again."

"The sun has not caught me in bed in fifty years."
 -- *Thomas Jefferson*

"I like my coffee black and my mornings bright."
 -- *Terri Guillemets*

"I used to love night best, but the older I get the more treasures and hope and joy I find in the mornings."

"Early morning cheerfulness can be extremely obnoxious"
-- *William Feather*

"Every morning you have 2 choices: continue to sleep with dreams or wake up and chase your dreams. The choice is yours!"

"Even after all this time the sun never says to the Earth: 'You owe me'."

"Lose an hour in the morning, and you will spend all day looking for it."
— *Richard Whately*

"Be willing to be a beginner every single morning."
-- *Meister Eckhart*

"Now that your eyes are open, make the sun jealous with your burning passion to start the day. Make the sun jealous or stay in bed."
— *Malak El Halabi*

"Smile in the mirror. Do that every morning and you'll start to see a big difference in your life."
— *Yoko Ono*

"You have to get up every morning and tell yourself 'I can do this'."

"Goooooooooaaaaaaal!"

"The reason most people never reach their goals is that they don't define them, or ever seriously consider them as believable or achievable. Winners can tell you where they are going, what they plan to do along the way, and who will be sharing the adventure with them."
 — *Denis Watley*

"You don't have to be a fantastic hero to do certain things to compete. You can be just an ordinary chap, sufficiently motivated to reach challenging goals."
 — *Edmund Hillary*

"Our goals can only be reached through a vehicle of a plan, in which we must fervently believe, and upon which we must vigorously act. There is no other route to success."
 — *Stephen A. Brennan*

"When we are motivated by goals that have deep meaning, by dreams that need completion, by pure love that needs expressing, then we truly live life."
 — *Greg Anderson*

"Goals are dreams with deadlines."
 — *Diana Scharf Hunt*

"Without goals, and plans to reach them, you are like a ship that has set sail with no destination."
— *Fitzhugh Dodson*

"I feel that the most important step in any major accomplishment is setting a specific goal. This enables you to keep your mind focused on your goal and off the many obstacles that will arise when you're striving to do your best."
— *Kurt Thomas*

"Life's up and downs provide windows of opportunity to determine your values and goals. Think of using all obstacles as stepping stones to build the life you want."
— *Marsha Sinetar*

"In life, as in football, you won't go far unless you know where the goalposts are."
— *Arnold H. Glasgow*

"Never look down to test the ground before taking your next step; only he who keeps his eye fixed on the far horizon will find his right road."
— *Dag Hammarskjold*

"You must have long term goals to keep you from being frustrated by short term failures."
— *Charles C. Noble*

"Obstacles are those frightful things you see when you take your eyes off your goals."
 — *Sydney Smith*

"My philosophy of life is that if we make up our mind what we are going to make of our lives, then work hard toward that goal, we never lose - somehow we win out"
 — *Ronald Reagan*

"Our plans miscarry because they have no aim. When a man does not know what harbor he is making for, no wind is the right wind."
 — *Seneca*

"Man is a goal seeking animal. His life only has meaning if he is reaching out and striving for his goals."
 — *Aristotle*

"If you're bored with life - you don't get up every morning with a burning desire to do things, you don't have enough goals."
 — *Lou Holtz*

"If one advances confidently in the direction of his dreams, and endeavors to live the life which he has imagined, he will meet with a success unexpected in common hours."
 — *Henry David Thoreau*

"You can't hit a home run unless you step up to the plate. You can't catch a fish unless you put your line in the water. You can't reach your goals if you don't try."
  – *Kathy Seligman*

"Crystallize your goals. Make a plan for achieving them and set yourself a deadline. Then, with supreme confidence, determination and disregard for obstacles and other people's criticisms, carry out your plan."
  – *Paul Meyer*

"The trouble with not having a goal is that you can spend your life running up and down the field and never score."
  – *Bill Copeland*

"Goals are not only absolutely necessary to motivate us. They are essential to really keep us alive."
  – *Robert H. Schuller*

"If you have a goal in life that takes a lot of energy, that requires a lot of work, that incurs a great deal of interest and that is a challenge to you, you will always look forward to waking up to see what the new day brings."
  – *Susan Polis Schultz*

"You have to set goals that are almost out of reach. If you set a goal that is attainable without much work or thought, you are stuck with something below your true talent and potential."
  – *Steve Garvey*

"Choosing a goal and sticking to it changes everything."
— *Scott Reed*

"The tragedy of life doesn't lie in not reaching your goal. The tragedy lies in having no goals to reach."
— *Benjamin Mays*

"Goals determine what you're going to be."
— *Julius Erving*

"Think little goals and expect little achievements. Think big goals and win big success."
— *David Joseph Schwartz*

"Progress has little to do with speed, but much to do with direction."
— *Author Unknown*

"Whoever wants to reach a distant goal must take small steps."
— *Helmut Schmidt*

"To achieve happiness, we should make certain that we are never without an important goal."
— *Earl Nightingale*

"The world makes way for the man who knows where he is going."
— *Ralph Waldo Emerson*

"When you determine what you want, you have made the most important decision in your life. You have to know what you want in order to attain it."

– Douglas Lurtan

"Great minds have purposes; others have dreams."

– Washington Irving

"You measure the size of the accomplishment by the obstacles you had to overcome to reach your goals."

– Booker T. Washington

"I learned that if you want to make it bad enough, no matter how bad it is, you can make it."

– Gale Sayers

"The most important thing about goals is having one."

– Geoffry F. Abert

"It takes a person with a mission to succeed."

– Clarence Thomas

"Set your goals high, and don't stop till you get there."

– Bo Jackson

"Be sure to take the most direct route to your dreams. Never take your eyes off your goal, or you will lose course. Never look back in sorrow, or you will trip."

– Joe Brown

"Success is the progressive realization of a worthy goal or ideal."
 — *Earl Nightingale*

"Your goals are the road maps that guide you and show you what is possible for your life."
 — *Les Brown*

"First say to yourself what you would be; and then do what you have to do."
 — *Epictetus*

"What you get by achieving your goals is not as important as what you become by achieving your goals."
 — *Zig Ziglar*

"The great thing in this world is not so much where we are, but in what direction we are moving."
 — *Oliver Wendell Holmes*

"It doesn't matter where you are coming from. All that matters is where you are going."
 — *Brian Tracy*

"By losing your goal, You have lost your way."
 — *Friedrich Nietzsche*

"You have to know what you want to get."
 — *Gertrude Stein*

"You've got to be very careful if you don't know where you are going, because you might not get there."
— *Yogi Berra*

"People with goals succeed because they know where they're going."
— *Earl Nightingale*

"Shoot for the moon, even if you miss, you'll land amongst the stars."
— *Les Brown*

"Goals help focus you on areas in both your personal and professional life that are important and meaningful, rather than being guided by what other people want you to be, do, or accomplish."
— *Catherine Pulsifer*

"The minute you choose to do what you really want to do it's a different kind of life."
 — *Buckminster Fuller*

"Think excitement, talk excitement, act out excitement, and you are bound to become an excited person. Life will take on a new zest, deeper interest and greater meaning. You can think, talk, and act yourself into dullness or into monotony or into unhappiness. By the same process you can build up inspiration, excitement and surging depth of joy."
 — *Norman Vincent Peale*

"In order to succeed, your desire for success should be greater than your fear of failure."
 — *Bill Cosby*

"Build up your weaknesses until they become your strong points."
 — *Knute Rockne*

"As you move through life, set aside good ideas and give them to others to encourage and inspire."
 — *Peter J. Daniels*

"Life is your business, and YOU are the boss."

"Talent alone won't make you a success. Neither will being in the right place at the right time, unless you are ready. The most important question is: Are your ready?"

— Johnny Carson

"You stop being average the day you decide to become a Champion, because the average person won't make that decision."

— Tom Hopkins

"You have to perform at a consistently higher level than others. That's the mark of a true professional."

— Joe Paterno

"My ability to concentrate and work toward that goal has been my greatest asset."

— Jack Nicklaus

"Dreams are where Achievements are born."

"Opportunity is not for those who can! Opportunity is for those who do!"

"Your own value is determined"
Not by what you are,
But what you are able to make out of yourself."

"Desire, dedication and discipline will win the day and the dream!"

Motivate Quotivate

"You win some, you lose some, and some get rained out, but you gotta suit up for them all."
 — *J. Askenberg*

"You've got to take the initiative and play your game. In a decisive set, confidence is the difference."
 — *Chris Evert*

"There are no shortcuts to any place worth going."
 — *Beverly Sills*

"If you don't have confidence, you'll always find a way not to win."
 — *Carl Lewis*

"You only ever grow as a human being if you're outside your comfort zone."
 — *Percy Cerutty*

"The turning point in the process of growing up is when you discover the core of strength within you that survives all hurt."
 — *Max Lerner*

"Train, don't strain."
 — *Arthur Lydiard*

"Spirit ... has fifty times the strength and staying power of brawn and muscle."
— *Unknown*

"It is only through work and strife that either nation or individual moves on to greatness. The great man is always the man of mighty effort, and usually the man whom grinding need has trained to mighty effort."
— *Theodore Roosevelt*, in a speech about Grant, delivered at Galena, Illinois, April 27, 1900

"Continuous effort — not strength or intelligence, is the key to unlocking our potential."
— *Liane Cardes*

"If you train hard, you'll not only be hard, you'll be hard to beat."
— *Herschel Walker*

"Number one is just to gain a passion for running. To love the morning, to love the trail, to love the pace on the track. And if some kid gets really good at it, that's cool too."
— *Pat Tyson*

"Just remember this: No one ever won the olive wreath with an impressive training diary."
— *Marty Liquori*

"Nothing will work unless you do."
— *John Wooden*

"You would fain be victor at the Olympic games, you say. Yes, but weigh the conditions, weigh the consequences; then and then only, lay to your hand-if it be for your profit. You must live by rule, submit to diet, abstain from dainty meats, exercise your body perforce at stated hours, in heat or in cold; drink no cold water, nor, it may be, wine. In a word, you must surrender yourself wholly to your trainer, as though to a physician."
— *Epictetus,* (c.A.D. 50-c.A.D. 138)

"The more I talk to athletes, the more convinced I become that the method of training is relatively unimportant. There are many ways to the top, and the training method you choose is just the one that suits you best. No, the important thing is the attitude of the athlete, the desire to get to the top."
— *Herb Elliott*

"Restlessness is discontent - and discontent is the first necessity of progress. Show me a thoroughly satisfied man - and I will show you a failure."
— *Thomas Alva Edison*

"The five S's of sports training are: stamina, speed, strength, skill, and spirit; but the greatest of these is spirit."
— *Ken Doherty*

"Fall seven times, stand up eight."
— *Japanese proverb*

"My jump was imperfect; my run-in was too short and my hands were too far back at takeoff. When I manage to iron out these faults, I am sure I can improve."
— *Sergei Bubka* (first pole vaulter to clear 20 feet)

"Only those who risk going to far can possibly find out how far one can go."
— *T.S. Eliot*

"Daring ideas are like chessmen moved forward; they may be beaten, but they may start a winning game."
— *Johann Wolfgang von Goethe*

"Man cannot discover new oceans unless he has the courage to lose sight of the shore."
— *Andre Gide*

"Inspiration cannot be willed, though it can be wooed."
— *Anthony Storr*

"Problems are only opportunities in work clothes."
— *Henry J. Kaiser*

"Only he who can see the invisible can do the impossible."
— *Frank L. Gaines*

"Everything you want is out there waiting for you to ask. Everything you want also wants you. But you have to take action to get it."
— *Jack Canfield*

"The difference between the impossible and the possible lies in a person's determination."
-- *Tommy Lasorda*

Motivational Moments

"When you are confused about your goal in life, let go of everything. Go deep within yourself and the answer will appear to you."

"In life, as well as in dance, grace glides on blistered feet."

"Dance is like life: it's beautiful, graceful and artistic, but you have to go through the pain and hard work to achieve your ultimate goal."

"If you look on the bright side of life, you will find enough to be cheerful and happy."

"The past belongs to the past. Let's focus on the big picture up front; let's focus in the future. Remember, what is on front of us is more important than what's left behind."

"Sometimes it is BEST for everyone you love to keep how you feel to yourself. You'll most likely get your chance in your next life and it will be a happier one than the previous one."

"I am certain that Life is uncertain, but with a strong Faith, you will make it through."

"Don't give up on Hope because Hope would never give up on you."

"It's sometimes good to be a dreamer, as long as you have the ability to turn those dreams into reality. Getting caught in the imaginary world may provide temporary happiness, getting back to reality is what is important. Stick to your dreams, share them and make the most out of them!"

"Your worth goes up a million when you shed tears and smile."

"True beauty is like art; it's something you see with your heart. Even a blind man can see true beauty and be moved by it."

"Our limitations in life do not lie in the midst of our abilities but lie in the positive attitude to see past our abilities."

"Life is too short to fall victim to our own emotions."

"It's true, hard work never killed anybody, but I figure, why take the chance?"
— *Ronald Reagan*

"I hope the millions of people I've touched have the optimism and desire to share their goals and hard work and persevere with a positive attitude."
— *Michael Jordan*

"Dictionary is the only place that success comes before work. Hard work is the price we must pay for success. I think you can accomplish anything if you're willing to pay the price."
— *Vince Lombardi*

"Football is like life - it requires perseverance, self-denial, hard work, sacrifice, dedication and respect for authority."
— *Vince Lombardi*

"The price of success is hard work, dedication to the job at hand, and the determination that whether we win or lose, we have applied the best of ourselves to the task at hand."
— *Vince Lombardi*

"Leaders aren't born they are made. And they are made just like anything else, through hard work. And that's the price we'll have to pay to achieve that goal, or any goal."
— *Vince Lombardi*

"I don't pity any man who does hard work worth doing. I admire him. I pity the creature who does not work, at whichever end of the social scale he may regard himself as being."
— *Theodore Roosevelt*

"John Kerry believes in an America where hard work is rewarded."
— *Barack Obama*

"The three great essentials to achieve anything worth while are: Hard work, Stick-to-itiveness, and Common sense."
— *Thomas A. Edison*

"There is no substitute for hard work."
— *Thomas A. Edison*

"The reason a lot of people do not recognize opportunity, is because it usually goes around wearing overalls looking like hard work."
— *Thomas A. Edison*

"Life grants nothing to us mortals without hard work."
— *Horace*

"I know you've heard it a thousand times before. But it's true - hard work pays off. If you want to be good, you have to practice, practice, practice. If you don't love something, then don't do it."

— Ray Bradbury

"Luck? I don't know anything about luck. I've never banked on it and I'm afraid of people who do. Luck to me is something else: Hard work - and realizing what is opportunity and what isn't."

— Lucille Ball

"Young people are threatened... by the evil use of advertising techniques that stimulate the natural inclination to avoid hard work by promising the immediate satisfaction of every desire."

— Pope John Paul II

"Nothing ever comes to one that is worth having, except as a result of hard work."

— Booker T. Washington

"Perseverance is the hard work you do after you get tired of doing the hard work you already did."

— Newt Gingrich

"Reform is not pleasant, but grievous; no person can reform themselves without suffering and hard work, how much less a nation."

— Thomas Carlyle

"Plans are only good intentions unless they immediately degenerate into hard work."
 – *Peter Drucker*

"What is success? I think it is a mixture of having a flair for the thing that you are doing; knowing that it is not enough, that you have got to have hard work and a certain sense of purpose."
 – *Margaret Thatcher*

Positive Attitude,
It Changes Everything.

"Great effort springs naturally from a great attitude."
— *Pat Riley*

"Like success, failure is many things to many people. With Positive Mental Attitude, failure is a learning experience, a rung on the ladder, a plateau at which to get your thoughts in order and prepare to try again."
— *W. Clement Stone*

"Your attitude, not your aptitude, will determine your altitude."
— *Zig Ziglar*

"Develop an attitude of gratitude, and give thanks for everything that happens to you, knowing that every step forward is a step toward achieving something bigger and better than your current situation."
— *Brian Tracy*

"You can adopt the attitude there is nothing you can do, or you can see the challenge as your call to action"
— *Catherine Pulsifer*

"You can do it if you believe you can!"
— *Napoleon Hill*

"An optimist is a person who sees a green light everywhere, while the pessimist sees only the red stoplight...
The truly wise person is colorblind."
 — *Albert Schweitzer*

"Positive thinking will let you do everything better than negative thinking will."
 — *Zig Ziglar*

"You cannot control what happens to you, but you can control your attitude toward what happens to you, and in that, you will be mastering change rather than allowing it to master you."
 — *Brian Tracy*

Shoot For The Moon

"Don't waste your time on jealousy. Sometimes you're ahead, sometimes you're behind. The race is long, and in the end it's only with yourself."

"Stop saying you've regrets in life. Just look at everything as a living and learning experience because you can change what you lived and learned."

"Look at each day as a chance to invest life into life. A chance to share your experience and deposit it into someone else's conscience. Each day is a chance to work miracles in the lives of others."

"It is never too late to correct a mistake especially if correction of that mistake leads to your happiness."

"I believe that you control your destiny, that you can be what you want to be. You can also stop and say, No, I won't do it, I won't behave his way anymore. I'm lonely and I need people around me, maybe I have to change my methods of behaving and then you do it."

"It's too easy to dare to be different, but too difficult to actually appreciate differences."

"Perhaps the most important thing we can undertake toward the reduction of fear is to make it easier for people to accept themselves, to like themselves."

"Concentration is a habit; you have to develop it. Performance is the state of mind; you have to perform like you are already a winner."

"You can choose whichever one you desire: Negative way ~Nothing I do matters; we're all going to die in the end. Positive way~ In life, everything matters; savor every second."

"Men walk through life and have many things to ponder. But this, above all, should leave no room to wonder - Who am I?"

"Success consists of a great heart, courageous mind and a kindred spirit lit by a fire that cannot be put out by the rough blows of the pessimist and the critic."

Connect the Dots

"If we want to feel an undying passion for our work, if we want to feel we are contributing to something bigger than ourselves, we all need to know our WHY."
 — *Simon Sinek,* Find Your Why: A Practical Guide for Discovering Purpose for You and Your Team

"I believe any company needs to have a foundation of Core Values. For BNI, they are Givers Gain, building business through meaningful relationships, training and education, traditions plus innovation and positive attitude."
 — *Norm Dominguez*

"Educate your network.
Make sure everyone in your network knows your clear, repeatable, memorable message and when to share it."
 — *Cys Bronner*

"We are not in a position in which we have nothing to work with. We already have capacities, talents, direction, missions, callings."
 — *Abraham Maslow*

"I'm a success today because I had a friend who believed in me and I didn't have the heart to let him down."
 — *Abraham Lincoln*

"Experience tells you what to do; confidence allows you to do it."
— *Stan Smith*

"Courage is a resistance to fear, mastery of fear – not absence of fear."
— *Mark Twain*

"Courage doesn't always roar. Sometimes courage is the quiet voice at the end of the day saying, 'I will try again tomorrow'."
— *Mary Anne Radmacher*

"You are braver than you believe, stronger than you seem, and smarter than you think."
— *Christopher Robin*

"No amount of security is worth the suffering of a life chained to a routine that has killed your dreams."
— *Unknown*

"Courage is simply the willingness to be afraid and act anyway."
— *Dr. Robert Anthony*

"Courage is not the absence of fear, but rather the judgment that something else is more important than fear."

 – *Ambrose Redmoon*

"I learned that courage was not the absence of fear, but the triumph over it. The brave man is not he who does not feel afraid, but he who conquers that fear."

 – *Nelson Mandela*

"Courage is the power to let go of the familiar."

 – *Raymond Lindquist*

"You have to have confidence in your ability, and then be tough enough to follow through."

 – *Rosalynn Carter*

"The way to develop self-confidence is to do the thing you fear."

 – *William Jennings Bryan*

"Confidence, like art, never comes from having all the answers; it comes from being open to all the questions."

 – *Earl Gray Stevens*

"Put all excuses aside and remember this: YOU are capable."

 – *Zig Ziglar*

"No matter who you are, no matter what you do, you absolutely, positively do have the power to change."
— *Bill Phillips*

"Don't wait until everything is just right. It will never be perfect. There will always be challenges, obstacles and less than perfect conditions. So what. Get started now. With each step you take, you will grow stronger and stronger, more and more skilled, more and more self-confident and more and more successful."
— *Mark Victor Hansen*

"Whatever course you decide upon, there is always someone to tell you that you are wrong. There are always difficulties arising which tempt you to believe that your critics are right. To map out a course of action and follow it to an end requires courage."
— *Ralph Waldo Emerson*

"Courage is fear that has said its prayers."
— *Dorothy Bernard*

Be Ambitious

"Cause Change & Lead. Accept Change & Survive. Resist Change & Die"
 -- *Ray Norda, Chairman, Novell*

"Remember: Success is nothing but luck. Just ask any failure."
 -- *Anon*

"If one does not know to which port one is sailing, no wind is favorable."
 -- *Seneca*

"Whatever the mind of man can conceive and believe, it can achieve."
 -- *Napoleon Hill*

"Real knowledge is to know the extent of one's ignorance."
 -- *Confucius*

"Eighty percent of success is showing up."
 -- *Woody Allen*

"Even if you are on the right track, you'll get run over if you just sit there!"
 -- *Will Rogers*

"Never Give Up"
 — *Winston Churchill*

"Winners never quit and quitters never win."
 — *Anon*

"Winners lose *much* more often than losers. So if you keep losing but you're still trying, keep it up! You're right on track."
 — *Matthew Keith Groves*

"Blessed are the flexible, for they shall not be bent out of shape."
 — *Anon*

"In the confrontation between the stream and the rock, the stream always wins - not through strength, but through persistence."
 — *Buddha*

"Who dares wins"
 — *Winston Churchill*

"Trust in yourself. Your perceptions are often far more accurate than you are willing to believe."
 — *Claudia Black*

"Imagination rules the world."
 — *Napoleon Bonaparte*

"If think you can't, you're right. If think you can, you're right."

— *Ken Hatton*

"Work like you don't need the money. Sing like nobody's listening, Dance like nobody's watching, Love like you've never been hurt, Live like Earth is Heaven."

— *Anon*

Quotes That Give You Altitude

"Attitude: It is our best friend or our worst enemy."
 — *John C. Maxwell*

"Your attitude determines your altitude!"
 — *Denis Waitley*

"A strong positive attitude will create more miracles than any wonder drug."
 — *Patricia Neal*

"The greatest revolution of our generation is the discovery that human beings, by changing the inner attitudes of their minds, can change the outer aspects of their lives."
 — *William James*

"The world of achievement has always belonged to the optimist."
 — *J. Harold Wilkins*

"If you change the way you look at things, the things you look at change."
 — *Wayne Dyer*

"You can complain that roses have thorns, or rejoice that thorns have roses."
 — *Ziggy*

"Nothing can stop the man with the right mental attitude from achieving his goal; nothing on earth can help the man with the wrong mental attitude."
— *Thomas Jefferson*

"It is our attitude at the beginning of a difficult task which, more than anything else, will affect its successful outcome."
— *William James*

"Life is 10% what happens to us and 90% how we react to it."
— *Dennis P. Kimbro*

"The last of the human freedoms is to choose one's attitude in any given set of circumstances."
— *Victor E. Frankl*

"Everyone faces defeat. It may be a stepping-stone or a stumbling block, depending on the mental attitude with which it is faced."
— *Napoleon Hill*

"Life is a grindstone. Whether it grinds us down or polishes us up depends on us."
— *Thomas L. Holdcroft*

"If you don't like something, change it. If you can't change it, change your attitude. Don't complain."
— *Maya Angelou*

"Progress is impossible without change and those who cannot change their minds cannot change anything."
— *George Bernard Shaw*

"If you change the way you look at things, the things you look at change."
— *Wayne Dyer*

"The difference between a mountain and a molehill is your perspective."
— *Al Neuharth*

Quotes of Note

"Behind an able man there are always other able men."
— *Chinese Proverb*

"Put yourself in a state of mind where you say to yourself,
"Here is an opportunity for you to celebrate like never
before, my own power, my own ability to get myself to
do whatever is necessary."
— *Anthony Robbins*

"Adversity has the effect of eliciting talents, which in
prosperous circumstances would have lain dormant."
— *Horace*

"There is something that is much more scarce, something
rarer than ability. It is the ability to recognize ability."
— *Robert Half*

"I think luck is the sense to recognize an opportunity and
the ability to take advantage of it... The man who can
smile at his breaks and grab his chances gets on."
— *Samuel Goldwyn*

"When I examine myself and my methods of thought, I
come to the conclusion that the gift of fantasy has meant
more to me than my talent for absorbing positive
knowledge."
— *Albert Einstein*

"Creativity is essentially a lonely art. An even lonelier struggle. To some a blessing. To others a curse. It is in reality the ability to reach inside yourself and drag forth from your very soul an idea."

-- *Lou Dorfsman*

"There are two kinds of talents, man-made talent and God-given talent. With man-made talent you have to work very hard. With God-given talent, you just touch it up once in a while."

-- *Pearl Bailey*

"Perhaps the most valuable result of all education is the ability to make yourself do the thing you have to do, when it ought to be done, whether you like it or not."

-- *Walter Bagehot*

"The greatest good we can do our country is to heal its party divisions and make them one people."
— *Thomas Jefferson*

"This is the miracle that happens every time to those who really love - the more they give, the more they possess."
— *Maria Rainer Rilke*

"Pace yourself...an elephant can be swallowed, one bite at a time"
— *Dana Bidne*

"Action may not always bring happiness, but there is no happiness without action."
— *Benjamin Disraeli*

"Nobody made a greater mistake than he who did nothing because he could do only a little."
— *Edmund Burke*

"You can't do anything about the length of your life, but you can do something about its width and depth."
— *Shira Tehrani*

"Well done is better than well said."
— *Benjamin Franklin*

"If the world seems cold to you, kindle fires to warm it."
— *Lucy Larcom*

Science may have found a cure for most evils; but it has found no remedy for the worst of them all — the apathy of human beings."
— *Helen Keller*

"Life is a great big canvas, and you should throw all the paint you can on it."
— *Danny Kaye*

"Bite off more than you can chew, then chew it."
— *Ella Williams*

"To live for results would be to sentence myself to continuous frustration. My only sure reward is in my actions and not from them."
— *Hugh Prather*

"Unless you're willing to have a go, fail miserably, and have another go, success won't happen."
— *Phillip Adams*

"It is our attitude at the beginning of a difficult task which, more than anything else, will affect It's successful outcome."
— *William James*

"I believe life is to be lived, not worked, enjoyed, not agonized, loved, not hated."
— *Leland Bartlett*

"The person who gets the farthest is generally the one who is willing to do and dare. The sure-thing boat never gets far from shore."
— *Dale Carnegie*

"Everyone who got where he is has had to begin where he was."
— *Robert Louis Stevenson*

"The gem cannot be polished without friction, nor man perfected without trials."
— *Chinese proverb*

Duty makes us do things well, but love makes us do them beautifully."
— *Zig Ziglar*

"A non-doer is very often a critic-that is, someone who sits back and watches doers, and then waxes philosophically about how the doers are doing. It's easy to be a critic, but being a doer requires effort, risk, and change."
— *Dr. Wayne W. Dyer*

"Do not be desirous of having things done quickly. Do not look at small advantages. Desire to have things done quickly prevents their being done thoroughly. Looking at small advantages prevents great affairs from being accomplished."
— *Confucius*

"The greater the difficulty the more glory in surmounting it. Skillful pilots gain their reputation from storms and tempests."
— *Epictetus*

"In order to succeed, you must first be willing to fail."
— *Anonymous*

"Don't limit yourself. Many people limit themselves to what they think they can do. You can go as far as your mind lets you. What you believe, remember, you can achieve."
— *Mary Kay Ash*

"Don't quack like a duck.. soar like an eagle."
— *Ken Blanchard*

"The turning point, I think, was when I really realized that you can do it yourself. That you have to believe in you because sometimes that's the only person that does believe in your success but you."
— *Tim Blixseth*

"The way to get started is to quit talking and begin doing."
— *Walt Disney*

"Follow your own particular dreams. We are handed a life by peers, parents and society, you can do that or follow your own dreams." "Life is short, be a dreamer but be a practical person."
— *Hugh Hefner*

"In spite of your fear, do what you have to do."
— *Chin-Ning Chu*

"When life appears to be working against you, when your luck is down, when the supposedly wrong people show up, or when you slip up and return to old, self-defeating habits, recognize the signs that you're out of harmony with intention."

— *Aldous Huxley*

Positive Charge

"Nothing can stop the man with the right mental attitude from achieving his goal; nothing on earth can help the man with the wrong mental attitude."

-- Thomas Jefferson

"Success is the sum of small efforts, repeated day in and day out."

-- Robert Collier

"The thing always happens that you really believe in; and the belief in a thing makes it happen."

-- Frank Loyd Wright

"A failure is a man who has blundered, but is not able to cash in on the experience."

-- Elbert Hubbard

"There is only one success --to be able to spend your life in your own way."

-- Christopher Morley

"Failures do what is tension relieving, while winners do what is goal achieving."

-- Dennis Waitley

"Success does not consist in never making blunders, but in never making the same one a second time."

-- Josh Billings

"The difference between a successful person and others is not a lack of strength, not a lack of knowledge, but rather a lack in will."
— *Vince Lombardi*

"Success is the good fortune that comes from aspiration, desperation, perspiration and inspiration."
— *Evan Esar*

"The talent of success is nothing more than doing what you can do, well."
— *Henry W. Longfellow*

"Try not to become a man of success but a man of value."
— *Albert Einstein*

"If at first you don't succeed, try, try again. Then quit. There's no use being a damn fool about it."
— *W.C. Fields*

"I cannot give you the formula for success, but I can give you the formula for failure —which is: Try to please everybody."
— *Herbert Bayard Swope*

"The secret of success in life is for a man to be ready for his opportunity when it comes."
— *Earl of Beaconsfield*

"To climb steep hills requires a slow pace at first."
— *Shakespeare*

Closing Quotes

"Opportunity is missed by most people because it is dressed in overalls and looks like work."
 -- *Thomas A Edison*

"Blessed are those who can give without remembering and take without forgetting."
 -- *Elizabeth Bibesco*

"Yesterday is history, tomorrow is a mystery. And today? Today is a gift. That's why we call it the present."
 -- *B. Olatunji*

"When you get to the end of the rope, tie a knot and hang on."
 -- *Franklin D Roosevelt*

"Your attitude, not your aptitude, determines your altitude."
 -- *Zig Ziglar*

"If you're going through hell, keep going."
 -- *Winston Churchill*

"The secret to success is to start from scratch and keep on scratching."
 -- *Dennis Green*

"Champions aren't made in gyms. Champions are made from something they have deep inside them a desire, a dream, a vision. They have to have the skill and the will. But the will must be stronger than the skill."

— Muhammad Ali

"Most of the important things in the world have been accomplished by people who have kept on trying when there seemed to be no hope at all."

— Dale Carnegie

"So many of our dreams at first seems impossible, then they seem improbable, and then, when we summon the will, they soon become inevitable."

— Christopher Reeve

"Hard work spotlights the character of people. Some turn up their sleeves. Some turn up their noses, and some don't turn up at all."

— Sam Ewing

"Many of life's failures are people who had not realized how close they were to success when they gave up."

— Thomas A Edison

"There are those who work all day. Those who dream all day. And those who spend an hour dreaming before setting to work to fulfill those dreams. Go into the third category because there's virtually no competition."

— Steven J Ross

"Our greatest glory is not in never falling, but in rising every time we fall."
 — *Confucious*

"The main thing is to keep the main thing the main thing."
 — *Stephen Covey*

"Efficiency is doing things right. Effectiveness is doing the right things."
 — *Peter Drucker*

Be Mindful

"To have integrity is also to have character which is also the easiest way to run into conflict with those without either."
— *Byron Pulsifer*

"Have the courage to say no. Have the courage to face the truth. Do the right thing because it is right. These are the magic keys to living your life with integrity."
— *Mark Twain*

"Integrity can be difficult to maintain in a world that demands you change with the wind."
— *Byron Pulsifer*

"Integrity is what we do, what we say, and what we say we do."
— *Don Galer*

"To have integrity means that you don't agree with everyone you meet, nor do you succumb to pressure to be something that is in direct conflict with your core ethics."
— *Byron Pulsifer*

"Love all, trust a few, do wrong to none."
— *William Shakespeare*

"There is no failure except in no longer trying."
— *Elbert Hubbard*

"We can be resentful of our age, or we can be grateful for having attained it."
 —*William Arthur Ward*

"Everyday many not be a good one, but there is something good in every day."
 —*Unknown Author*

"People of mediocre ability sometimes achieve outstanding success because they don't know when to quit. Most men succeed because they are determined to."
 —*George Allen*

"Any fact facing us is not as important as our attitude toward it, for that determines our success or failure."
 —*Norman Vincent Peale*

"I studied the lives of great men and famous women, and I found that the men and women who got to the top were those who did the jobs they had in hand, with everything they had of energy and enthusiasm."
 —*Henry Truman*

"Good actions give strength to ourselves and inspire good actions in others."
  — *Plato*

"Are you in earnest? Seize this very minute! Boldness has genius, power, & magic in it. Only engage, and then the mind grows heated. Begin, and then the work will be completed."
  — *Jean Anouilh*

"Doing is a quantum leap from imagining. Thinking about swimming isn't much like actually getting in the water. Actually getting in the water can take your breath away. The defense force inside of us wants us to be cautious, to stay away from anything as intense as a new kind of action. Its job is to protect us, and it categorically avoids anything resembling danger. But it's often wrong. Anything worth doing is worth doing too soon."
  — *Barbara Sher*

"The time at our disposal each day is elastic; the passions we feel dilate it, those that inspire us shrink it, and habit fills it."
  — *Marcel Proust*

"All of us might wish at times that we lived in a more tranquil world, but we don't. And if our times are difficult and perplexing, so are they challenging and filled with opportunity."

-- Robert Kennedy

"Everyone has a responsibility to not only tolerate another person's point of view, but also to accept it eagerly as a challenge to your own understanding. And express those challenges in terms of serving other people."

-- Arlo Guthrie

"Coaches who can outline plays on a black board are a dime a dozen. The ones who win, get inside their player and motivate."

-- Vince Lombardi

"If your actions inspire others to dream more, learn more, do more and become more, you are a leader."

-- John Quincy Adams

"Your mind is a treasure house that you should stock well and it's the one part of you the world can't interfere with."

-- TIS by Frank McCourt

Action Quotes

"I've missed more than 9000 shots in my career. I've lost almost 300 games. 26 times, I've been trusted to take the game winning shot and missed. I've failed over and over and over again in my life. And that is why I succeed."
— Michael Jordan

Doctors and scientists said that breaking the four-minute mile was impossible, that one would die in the attempt. Thus, when I got up from the track after collapsing at the finish line, I figured I was dead."
— *Roger Bannister* (After becoming the first person to break the four-minute mile, 1952)

"Flaming enthusiasm, backed by horse sense and persistence, is the quality that most frequently makes for success."
— *Dale Carnegie*

"Champions aren't made in the gyms. Champions are made from something they have deep inside them — a desire, a dream, a vision."
— *Muhammad Ali*

"Champions keep playing until they get it right."
— *Billy Jean King*

"When I step onto the court, I don't have to think about anything. If I have a problem off the court, I find that after I play, my mind is clearer and I can come up with a better solution. It's like therapy. It relaxes me and allows me to solve problems."
 —*Michael Jordan*

"I don't measure a man's success by how high he climbs but how high he bounces when he hits bottom."
 — *General George S. Patton*

"For me, winning isn't something that happens suddenly on the field when the whistle blows and the crowds roar. Winning is something that builds physically and mentally every day that you train and every night that you dream."
 — *Emmitt Smith*

"My thoughts before a big race are usually pretty simple. I tell myself: Get out of the blocks, run your race, stay relaxed. If you run your race, you'll win... channel your energy. Focus."
 — *Carl Lewis*

"Do not confuse motion and progress. A rocking horse keeps moving but does not make any progress."
 — *Alfred A. Montapert*

"A good hockey player plays where the puck is. A great hockey player plays where the puck is going to be."
 — *Wayne Gretzky*

63 | Quotivate!

Genius Quotes

Albert Einstein was more than just a scientist.
Here are 25 amazing life lessons coming from the man himself!

1. "Intellectual growth should commence at birth and cease only at death."

2. "Everyone should be respected as an individual, but no one idolized."

3. "Never do anything against conscience even if the state demands it."

4. "If people are good only because they fear punishment, and hope for reward, then we are a sorry lot indeed."

5. "A perfection of means, and confusion of aims, seems to be our main problem."

6. "Love is a better teacher than duty."

7. "If you can't explain it simply, you don't understand it well enough."

8. "No problem can be solved from the same level of consciousness that created it."

9. "Insanity: doing the same thing over and over again and expecting different results."

10."Learn from yesterday, live for today, hope for tomorrow."

11."It has become appallingly obvious that our technology has exceeded our humanity."

12."Everything that can be counted does not necessarily count; everything that counts cannot necessarily be counted."

13."Force always attracts men of low morality."

14."Everything should be as simple as it is, but not simpler."

15."A man should look for what is, and not for what he thinks should be."

16."Any man who reads too much and uses his own brain too little falls into lazy habits of thinking."

17."A person who never made a mistake, never tried anything new."

18."It is the supreme art of the teacher to awaken joy in creative expression and knowledge."

19."Anyone who doesn't take truth seriously in small matters cannot be trusted in large ones either."

20. "Great spirits have always encountered violent opposition from mediocre minds."

21. "Education is what remains after one has forgotten what one has learned in school."

22. "Logic will get you from A to B. Imagination will take you everywhere."

23. "Anger dwells only in the bosom of fools."

24. "Information is not knowledge."

25. "Never lose a holy curiosity."

Meet Cys Bronner, Constant Social Media Networker & BNI Executive Director

Cys Bronner is the Founder of ActionSteps4Success and Executive Director and CRO (Chief Referral Officer) of BNI4Success, BNI's Greater Los Angeles leading Business Networking Organization. Not new to marketing, word-of-mouth, social media or otherwise, she has produced and participated in high profile webcast events such as The Grammys, The 1996 Summer Olympics in Atlanta, Former President Jimmy Carter at the UN Summit in Turkey, and interviews with Nelson Mandela, the late science fiction writer Douglas Adams (*A Hitchiker's Guide To The Galaxy*), and Metallica – but not all at once.

Living in Los Angeles, California with her husband and business partner Dave Rittenhouse, she passionately shares her Networking Success Steps and makes a killer brisket!

BNI4Success Podcasts
with Cys Bronner

The Voice of BNI Greater Los Angeles;
Where we'll talk about referral networking
that works!

BNIPodcast4Success.com

BNi.

Made in the USA
Middletown, DE
07 October 2022

12069376R00044